This Workbook Belongs to:

_____

Other workbooks from our library for your 2nd grader

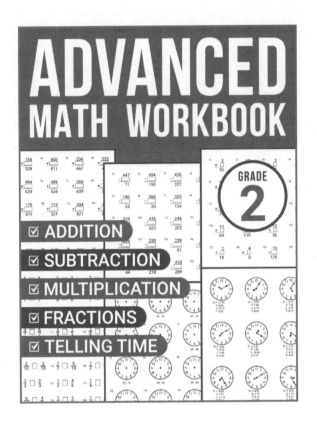

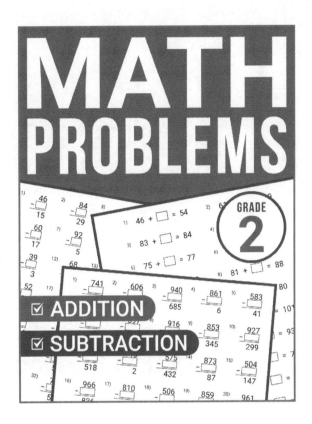

Scan the QR code below:

Scan the QR code below:

www.Nermilio.com

Table of Contents

Part 1

Adding 1 and 2-digit numbers (sums to 99)

Tim went to the store and bought 19 ice cream cones. He also won 33 more from a carnival game. How many ice cream cones does he have now?

$$\left(\right) = \bigcirc$$

A girl has 9 balloons, how many more balloons does she need to have to reach 36 balloons?

$$\left(\right) = \bigcirc$$

John has 26 marbles. His sister gives him 24 more marbles. He also finds 7 more marbles in the yard. How many marbles does he have now?

$$\left(\right) = \bigcirc$$

There are 36 pencils in the pencil box. Mary adds 7 more pencils. Timmy also adds 22 more pencils. How many pencils are in the pencil box now?

$$\left(\right) = \bigcirc$$

Sarah found 8 seashells on the beach. She also found 5 more shells on her next beach trip. How many seashells does she have now?

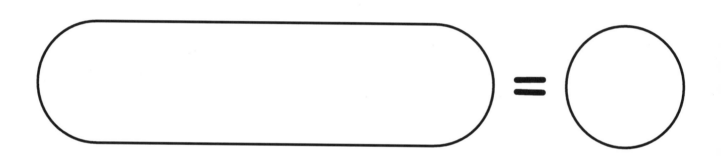

The store has 30 apples. They receive a delivery of 15 more apples. They also sell 5 apples to a customer. How many apples do they have now?

There are 35 books on the shelf. Emily adds 10 more books. The library also donates 5 books. How many books are on the shelf now?

$$\left(\right) = \bigcirc$$

A girl has 8 candy pieces, how many more candy pieces does she need to have to reach 12 candy pieces?

$$\left(\right) = \bigcirc$$

Michael has 16 toy cars, his friend gave him 4 more cars and he found 29 more cars in his neighbor's garage. How many toy cars does he have now?

$$(\quad) = (\quad)$$

The museum has 15 paintings. They receive a donation of 58 more paintings. They also purchase 13 paintings at an art show. How many paintings are at the museum now?

$$(\quad) = (\quad)$$

There are 30 stickers in the sticker book. Tom adds an additional 8 stickers. Timmy also gives him 15 stickers. How many stickers are in the sticker book now?

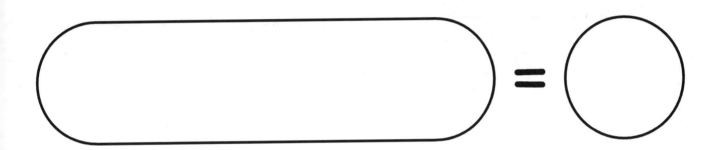

12. A boy has 24 kites, how many more kites does he need to have to reach 66 kites?

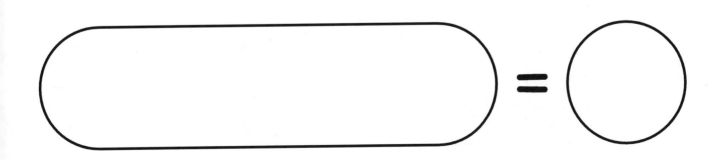

Samantha has 16 crayons. She found 24 more crayons in her sister's room and her mother bought her 32 more crayons. How many crayons does Samantha have now?

$$\left(\right) = \bigcirc$$

There are 20 birds in the park. 4 more birds fly into the park. Timmy also sees 16 birds flying over the park. How many birds are in the park now?

$$\left(\right) = \bigcirc$$

There are 25 flowers in the garden. Susan plants an additional 16 flowers. Ben also picks 43 flowers from the garden. How many flowers are in the garden now?

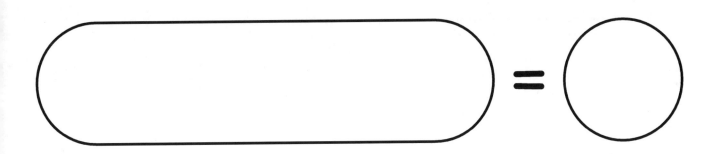

There are 30 students in the classroom. 54 more students join the class. The teacher also adds 12 more students to the class. How many students are in the classroom now?

A girl has 17 seashells. How many more seashells does she need to find to reach 32 seashells?

$$\Big(\Big) = \bigcirc$$

Emily has 4 balloons. She received 3 more balloons on her birthday and she bought 2 more balloons at a street fair. How many balloons does she have now?

$$\Big(\Big) = \bigcirc$$

The zoo has 18 animals. They receive a delivery of 9 more animals. They also receive a donation of 3 animals from a local petting zoo. How many animals are at the zoo now?

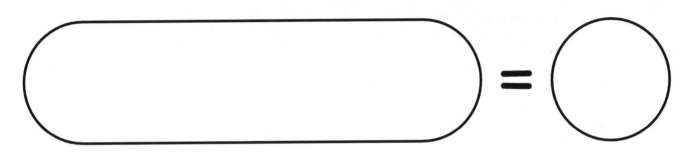

There are 20 dogs at the dog park. 7 more dogs come to the park. Lucas also sees 3 dogs being walked nearby. How many dogs are at the dog park now?

A boy catches 13 fish, how many more fish does he need to catch to reach 88 fish?

$$\left(\right) = \bigcirc$$

The store has 15 toys. They receive a shipment of 17 more toys. They also sell 33 toys to a customer. How many toys do they have now?

$$\left(\right) = \bigcirc$$

Daniel has 5 toy trains. He received 12 more toy trains from his grandfather and he found 13 more toy trains in a toy chest. How many toy trains does Daniel have now?

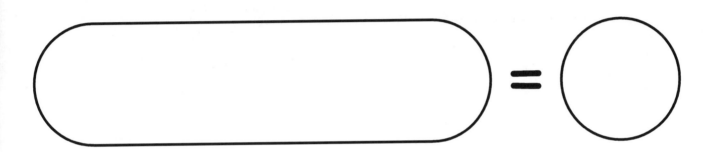

The library has 25 books. They receive a donation of 16 more books. They also purchase 23 books at a book sale. How many books are at the library now?

Ethan has 52 toy robots. He received 12 more toy robots from his grandparents and he found 5 more toy robots in the park. How many toy robots does Ethan have now?

$$\left(\right) = \bigcirc$$

Jake has 18 kites. He received 23 more kites as a gift and he made 5 more kites. How many kites does Jake have in total?

$$\left(\right) = \bigcirc$$

Jacob has 6 toy dinosaurs, how many more toy dinosaurs does he need to have to reach 59 dinosaurs?

$$\left(\right) = \bigcirc$$

Samuel has 16 crayons. He found 6 more crayons in his sister's room and his mother bought him 32 more crayons. How many crayons does Samuel have in total?

$$\left(\right) = \bigcirc$$

Evelyn has 25 jigsaw puzzles. She received 8 more jigsaw puzzles from her aunt and she bought 9 more jigsaw puzzles at a garage sale. How many jigsaw puzzles does Evelyn have now?

$$\Big(\qquad\qquad\Big) = \bigcirc$$

The school has 28 students. 33 more students enroll in the school. The teacher also adds 7 more students to the class. How many students are at the school now?

$$\Big(\qquad\qquad\Big) = \bigcirc$$

Scarlett has 5 marbles, how many more marbles does she need to have to reach 47 marbles?

( ) = ◯

Luke has 6 toy boats. He received 24 more toy boats from his cousin and he found 22 more toy boats at the lake. How many toy boats does Luke have now?

( ) = ◯

Chloe has 6 teddy bears. She received 9 more teddy bears from her neighbor and she bought 8 more teddy bears at a street fair. How many teddy bears does Chloe have in total?

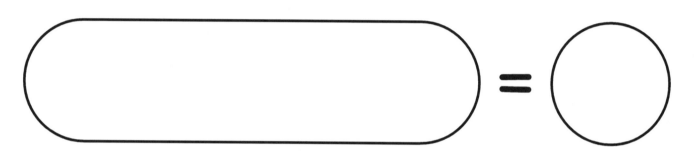

Matthew has 9 toy airplanes. He received 9 more toy airplanes from Julian, and he found 8 more toy airplanes in the sandbox. How many toy airplanes does Matthew have now?

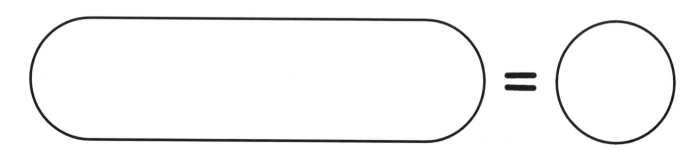

Madison has 18 cookies. She received 15 more cookies as a prize and she bought 39 more cookies at a store. How many cookies does Madison have in total?

$$\Big(\qquad\qquad\Big) = \bigcirc$$

Gabriel has 71 stickers. He received 15 more stickers as a prize and he bought 3 more stickers at a store. How many stickers does Gabriel have now?

$$\Big(\qquad\qquad\Big) = \bigcirc$$

Part 2

Adding numbers under 1,000

Kevin has 178 stickers and Emily has 36 stickers. How many stickers do they have together?

The ice cream shop sold 236 cones today and 402 cones yesterday. How many cones did they sell in total?

Mary has $189 and Jack has $221. How much money do they have together?

$$\left(\right) = \bigcirc$$

The museum has 563 paintings and the gallery has 345 paintings. How many paintings do they have in total?

$$\left(\right) = \bigcirc$$

The store has 138 apples and 552 oranges. How many fruits do they have in total?

$$\left(\right) = \bigcirc$$

The library has 84 books and the school has 412 books. How many books do they have in total?

$$\left(\right) = \bigcirc$$

There are 123 trees in the park and 456 trees in the forest. How many trees are there in total?

$$\Big(\qquad\qquad\Big) = \bigcirc$$

Anthony has 303 marbles and Dylan has 69 marbles. How many marbles do they have together?

$$\Big(\qquad\qquad\Big) = \bigcirc$$

Grace has 21 red pens and 14 blue pens. How many pens does Grace have in total?

$$\Big(\qquad\qquad\Big) = \Big(\quad\Big)$$

The park has 605 trees and the garden has 88 trees. How many trees are there in total?

$$\Big(\qquad\qquad\Big) = \Big(\quad\Big)$$

A monkey has 112 bananas. He finds 67 more in the jungle. How many bananas does the monkey have now?

$$\left(\right) = \bigcirc$$

Zoey has 15 strawberries in her basket. She picks 10 more in the garden. How many strawberries does Zoey have now?

$$\left(\right) = \bigcirc$$

Mary has 66 stickers and Emily has 324 stickers. How many stickers do they have together?

$$\left(\right) = \bigcirc$$

The store has 247 bananas and the market has 201 bananas. How many bananas are there in total?

$$\left(\right) = \bigcirc$$

Thomas has 504 baseball cards and he just got a package of 19 more in the mail. How many baseball cards does Thomas have now?

$$\left(\right) = \bigcirc$$

Charles has 890 legos and he got a big box of 56 more from her cousin. How many legos does Charles have now?

$$\left(\right) = \bigcirc$$

Victoria has 646 pencils and she went shopping and bought a box of 204. How many pencils does Victoria have now?

$$\left(\right) = \bigcirc$$

A monkey has 215 grapes, he finds 320 more in the jungle, and his friend gives him 33. How many grapes does the monkey have now?

$$\left(\right) = \bigcirc$$

A farmer has 408 watermelons in his farm, he harvests 140 more, and buys 109 from another farm. How many watermelons does he have now?

$$\Large\left(\quad\quad\quad\quad\right) = \bigcirc$$

Hannah has 114 cookies, she bakes 89 more and she gets 105 from Everly. How many cookies does she have now?

$$\Large\left(\quad\quad\quad\quad\right) = \bigcirc$$

Naomi has 50 apples, she picks 40 more from the tree, and buys 30 from the market. How many apples does Naomi have now?

$$\left(\right) = \bigcirc$$

Natalie found 308 coins in her piggy bank. Her neighbor gave her 55 more, and her brother gave her 118 more. How many coins does Natalie have now?

$$\left(\right) = \bigcirc$$

Andrew has 96 stickers and he won 186 more in a contest and bought 555 more from a store. How many stickers does Andrew have now?

$$(\qquad) = \bigcirc$$

Joshua has 129 marbles and he just found a bag with 777 more while on a hike and bought 16 more from a store. How many marbles does Joshua have now?

$$(\qquad) = \bigcirc$$

Cameron has 674 blocks, his parents gave him 70 for his birthday and he bought 66 more. How many blocks does Cameron have now?

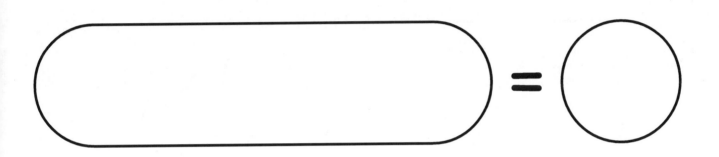

Audrey went to a candy store and bought 297 candies, but her neighbor gave her 49 and her parents gave her 99 more. How many candies does Audrey have now?

Christian has 90 crayons, but he received a gift of 700 and bought 16 more. How many crayons does Christian have now?

$$(\qquad) = \bigcirc$$

A boy has 210 cookies, his mom bakes him 115 more, and he gets 59 from his friend. How many cookies does he have now?

$$(\qquad) = \bigcirc$$

The school has 582 students and the university has 334 students. How many students are there in total?

$$\left(\quad\quad\quad\quad \right) = \bigcirc$$

Jonathan has $356 and Robert has $434. How much money do they have together?

$$\left(\quad\quad\quad\quad \right) = \bigcirc$$

A farmer has 319 apples in his orchard, he picks 247 more from his trees, and buys 188 from the market. How many apples does he have now?

$$\left(\right) = \bigcirc$$

Delilah has 5 carrots in her garden, she pulls 8 more from the ground, and buys 10 from the farmer's market. How many carrots does Delilah have now?

$$\left(\right) = \bigcirc$$

The store has 426 peaches and the market has 391 peaches. How many peaches are there in total?

$$\Big(\qquad\qquad\Big) = \bigcirc$$

Madelyn has 159 toys, but her grandparents gave her 287 more and her aunt gave her 94 more. How many toys does Madelyn have now?

$$\Big(\qquad\qquad\Big) = \bigcirc$$

he store has 761 lemons and the market has 224 lemons. How many apples are there in total?

$$\Big(\quad\Big) = \bigcirc$$

Hailey has $529 and Caroline has $356. How much money do they have together?

$$\Big(\quad\Big) = \bigcirc$$

Part 3

Subtracting 1 and 2-digit numbers

Allison has 56 stickers and gave away 9 stickers. How many stickers does Allison have left?

$$\left(\qquad\right) = \left(\quad\right)$$

The store had 35 apples and sold 12 apples. How many apples are left?

$$\left(\qquad\right) = \left(\quad\right)$$

Wesley has $87 and spent $29. How much money does Wesley have left?

$$\left(\right) = \bigcirc$$

The school had 68 students and 32 students left. How many students are left?

$$\left(\right) = \bigcirc$$

Jeremiah has 78 marbles and lost 23 marbles. How many marbles does Jeremiah have left?

$$\left(\right) = \bigcirc$$

The museum had 53 paintings and removed 45 paintings. How many paintings are left?

$$\left(\right) = \bigcirc$$

Anna has 89 stickers and gave away 34 stickers. How many stickers does Anna have left?

$$\Big(\Big) = \bigcirc$$

The store had 73 oranges and sold 42 oranges. How many oranges are left?

$$\Big(\Big) = \bigcirc$$

Ariana has $21 and spent $18. How much money does Ariana have left?

$$\Big(\qquad\qquad\Big) = \bigcirc$$

The park had 79 trees and cut down 30 trees. How many trees are left?

$$\Big(\qquad\qquad\Big) = \bigcirc$$

Jade has 98 stickers and gave away 67 stickers. How many stickers does Jade have left?

$$\Big(\Big) = \bigcirc$$

The school had 49 books and donated 12 books. How many books are left?

$$\Big(\Big) = \bigcirc$$

Nicholas has 87 marbles and lost 23 marbles. How many marbles does Nicholas have left?

$$\Big(\qquad\qquad\Big) = \Big(\quad\Big)$$

The store had 87 bananas and sold 9 bananas. How many bananas are left?

$$\Big(\qquad\qquad\Big) = \Big(\quad\Big)$$

Parker has $38 and spent $15. How much money does Parker have left?

$$\left(\right) = \bigcirc$$

The garden had 39 trees and removed 24 trees. How many trees are left?

$$\left(\right) = \bigcirc$$

Connor has 45 stickers and gave away 21 stickers. How many stickers does Connor have left?

$$\boxed{} = \bigcirc$$

The university had 94 students and graduated 32 students. How many students are left?

$$\boxed{} = \bigcirc$$

Sarah has 73 marbles and lost 29 marbles. How many marbles does Sarah have left?

( ) = ( )

Adam had 68 toy cars, but he gave 33 of them to his friend. How many toy cars does he have now?

( ) = ( )

Madeline had 77 apples, but she used 31 of them to make apple pie. How many apples does Madeline have left?

$$(\qquad) = \bigcirc$$

Damian had 87 marbles, but he traded 55 of them for some toy cars. How many marbles does Damian have now?

$$(\qquad) = \bigcirc$$

Eva had 91 stickers, but her little brother took 73 of them. How many stickers does Eva have left?

$$\Large\boxed{} = \bigcirc$$

Luka had 85 pieces of candy, but he gave 41 of them to his sister. How many pieces of candy does Luka have now?

$$\Large\boxed{} = \bigcirc$$

Clara had 54 crayons, but she lost 22 of them at school. How many crayons does Clara have now?

$$\left(\right) = \bigcirc$$

Vincent had 80 cookies, but he shared 7 of them with his classmates. How many cookies does Vincent have now?

$$\left(\right) = \bigcirc$$

Samantha had 55 dolls, but she gave 52 of them to her little sister. How many dolls does Samantha have now?

( ) = ( )

Maria had 9 balloons, but she gave 3 of them to her friends at her birthday party. How many balloons does Maria have now?

( ) = ( )

Myles had 12 legos, but he used 4 of them to build a spaceship. How many legos does Myles have now?

$$\left(\right) = \bigcirc$$

Iris had 7 stuffed animals, but she gave 2 of them to her cousin. How many stuffed animals does Iris have now?

$$\left(\right) = \bigcirc$$

Diego had 83 puzzle pieces, but he lost 5 of them. How many puzzle pieces does Diego have now?

$$\left(\right) = \bigcirc$$

Eliza had 18 books, but she gave 8 of them to the library. How many books does Eliza have now?

$$\left(\right) = \bigcirc$$

Nathaniel had 58 blocks, but he used 43 of them to build a tower. How many blocks does Nathaniel have now?

$$\boxed{} = \bigcirc$$

George had 84 toy cars, but he lost 65 of them at the park. How many toy cars does George have now?

$$\boxed{} = \bigcirc$$

Lorenzo had 16 marbles, but he lost 6 of them at the playground. How many marbles does Lorenzo have now?

$$\bigcirc = \bigcirc$$

Julia had 81 apples, but she used 2 of them to make apple juice. How many apples does Julia have now?

$$\bigcirc = \bigcirc$$

Part 4

Subtracting numbers below 1,000

The park had 632 benches and 23 benches were damaged. How many benches are left?

$\boxed{} = \bigcirc$

A bakery has 798 cookies and sells 56, how many cookies are left?

$\boxed{} = \bigcirc$

If you have 388 pencils and lose 194, how many pencils do you have left?

$$\Big(\ \ \ \ \ \ \ \ \ \Big) = \bigcirc$$

John has 781 pencils and gave away 423 pencils to his friend. How many pencils does John have left?

$$\Big(\ \ \ \ \ \ \ \ \ \Big) = \bigcirc$$

The school had 784 students and 58 students transferred to another school. How many students are left?

$$\boxed{} = \bigcirc$$

Kim has 561 stickers and gave away 123 stickers to her friend. How many stickers does Kim have left?

$$\boxed{} = \bigcirc$$

Rachel had $956 and spent $29 on a new shirt. How much money does Rachel have left?

( ) = ( )

The store had 738 oranges and sold 402 oranges to customers. How many oranges are left?

( ) = ( )

The store had 897 bananas and sold 312 bananas to customers. How many bananas are left?

( ) = ( )

Mary has $136 and spent $9 on a new pen. How much money does Mary have left?

( ) = ( )

The museum had 456 artifacts and 245 artifacts were lent to another museum. How many artifacts are left?

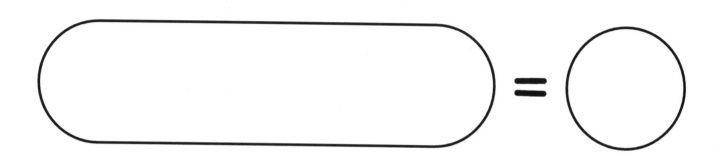

Sarah has 589 stickers and used 34 stickers to decorate her notebook. How many stickers does Sarah have left?

The school had 492 books and donated 182 books to the library. How many books are left?

$$\Big(\quad\quad\quad\quad\Big) = \bigcirc$$

The park had 791 trees and cut down 309 trees due to a storm. How many trees are left?

$$\Big(\quad\quad\quad\quad\Big) = \bigcirc$$

Jack has $438 and spent $15 on a new toy. How much money does Jack have left?

( ) = ( )

The garden had 309 trees and removed 102 trees due to a disease. How many trees are left?

( ) = ( )

The university had 812 students and graduated 638 students at the end of the semester. How many students are left?

$$\Big(\Big) = \bigcirc$$

If a store has 558 apples and sells 312, how many apples are left?

$$\Big(\Big) = \bigcirc$$

A school has 724 students but 132 are absent, how many students are present?

( ) = ( )

A toy box has 689 cars and you take away 245, how many cars are left?

( ) = ( )

A farmer has 975 chickens and sells 648, how many chickens are left?

$$\Big(\qquad\qquad\Big) = \bigcirc$$

A circus has 821 visitors and 712 left, how many visitors are remaining?

$$\Big(\qquad\qquad\Big) = \bigcirc$$

A museum has 761 artifacts and loans out 348, how many artifacts are left in the museum?

$$\Big(\Big) = \Big(\Big)$$

If a train has 540 passengers and 115 get off, how many passengers are left on the train?

$$\Big(\Big) = \Big(\Big)$$

A factory has 834 parts and loses 576 in a fire, how many parts are left?

$$\left(\right) = \bigcirc$$

A store has 952 items and sells 682, how many items are left?

$$\left(\right) = \bigcirc$$

If you have 166 cookies and your sister takes 83, how many cookies do you have left?

$$\left(\right) = \bigcirc$$

A company has 653 projects and completes 478, how many projects are left?

$$\left(\right) = \bigcirc$$

If you have 405 toy cars and give away 233, how many toy cars do you have left?

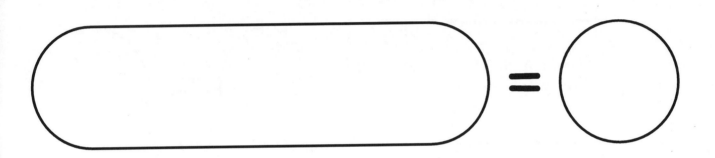

If you have 401 crayons and your friend borrows 318, how many crayons do you have left?

If a park has 551 benches and 69 are broken, how many benches are usable?

$$\left(\right) = \bigcirc$$

Mary has 373 marbles and lost 77 marbles while playing marbles with her friends. How many marbles does Mary have left?

$$\left(\right) = \bigcirc$$

If a store has 825 toys and sells 391, how many toys are left in the store?

$$\Large(\qquad\qquad\qquad) = \bigcirc$$

A park has 638 trees and loses 197 in a storm, how many trees are left?

$$\Large(\qquad\qquad\qquad) = \bigcirc$$

A library has 714 books and donates 249, how many books are left in the library?

( ) = ( )

If a store has 761 shirts and sells 216, how many shirts are left?

( ) = ( )

Part 5

Multiplication
(numbers to 50)

There are 9 cats in the pet store. Each cat has 4 legs. How many legs do all the cats have in total?

( ) = ( )

A toy store has 3 shelves. Each shelf has 5 toys on it. How many toys are there in the store in total?

( ) = ( )

A farmer has 5 fields with 4 rows of corn in each field. How many rows of corn are there in total?

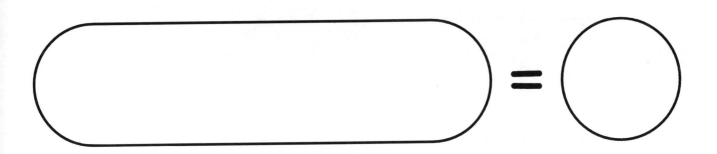

A baker has 3 batches of cookies. Each batch has 7 cookies. How many cookies does the baker have in total?

A class has 9 students. Each student has 2 hands. How many hands are there in the class in total?

$$\left(\right) = \bigcirc$$

There are 5 birds on a wire. Each bird has 2 wings. How many wings are there on the wire in total?

$$\left(\right) = \bigcirc$$

A toy box has 7 cars in it. Each car has 4 wheels. How many wheels are there in the toy box in total?

There are 4 tables in the classroom. Each table has 3 chairs. How many chairs are there in the classroom in total?

A zoo has 9 monkeys. Each monkey has 2 hands. How many hands are there in the zoo in total?

( ) = ( )

A deck of cards has 6 sets of 4 cards. How many cards are there in total?

( ) = ( )

There are 9 ducks in a pond. Each duck has 2 wings. How many wings are there in the pond in total?

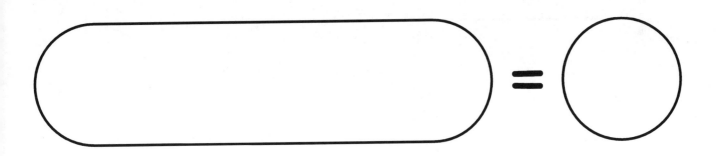

A school has 4 classrooms. Each classroom has 6 desks. How many desks are there in the school in total?

There are 6 books on a shelf. Each book has 8 pages. How many pages are there in total?

$$\Big(\qquad\qquad\Big) = \bigcirc$$

A toy store has 3 shelves. Each shelf has 6 toys on it. If you buy one toy from each shelf, how many toys will you have in total?

$$\Big(\qquad\qquad\Big) = \bigcirc$$

If 6 children each have 4 apples, how many apples do they have in total?

$$\Large\text{(} \qquad\qquad\qquad \text{)} = \bigcirc$$

If the Smith family has 9 chickens, how many eggs would they get if each chicken lays 2 eggs a day?

$$\Large\text{(} \qquad\qquad\qquad \text{)} = \bigcirc$$

If a farmer has 4 cows, and each cow produces 4 gallons of milk a day, how many gallons of milk does the farmer have in total?

( ) = ( )

If a plumber uses 3 pipes to repair a sink, and each pipe is 5 feet long, how many feet of pipe did the plumber use?

( ) = ( )

If there are 7 children playing with a soccer ball, and each child kicks the ball 3 times, how many kicks were there in total?

( ) = ( )

If a restaurant has 10 tables, and each table seats 6 people, how many people can the restaurant seat in total?

( ) = ( )

If a teacher has 7 students in her class, and each student has 7 pencils, how many pencils does the teacher have in total?

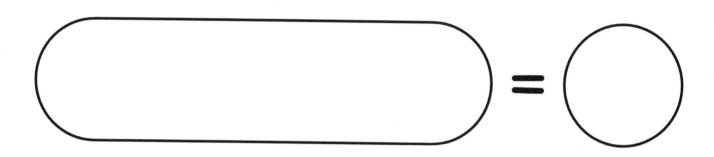

If a family is going on a picnic, and they take 8 sandwiches, and each sandwich is cut into 4 pieces, how many pieces of the sandwich will they have in total?

If a baker has 9 cakes, and each cake has 5 pieces, how many pieces of cake does the baker have in total

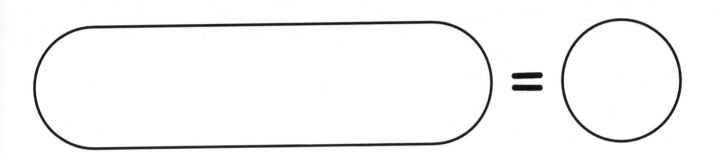

If a family has 16 bicycles, and each bike has 2 tires, how many tires does the family have in total?

A jar has 7 buttons in it. Each button has 4 holes. How many holes are there in the jar in total?

( ) = ( )

If a bakery makes 12 cakes per day and each cake sells for $15, how much money does the bakery make per day?

( ) = ( )

If a restaurant serves 13 customers per hour and each customer orders 2 drinks, how many drinks does the restaurant serve per hour?

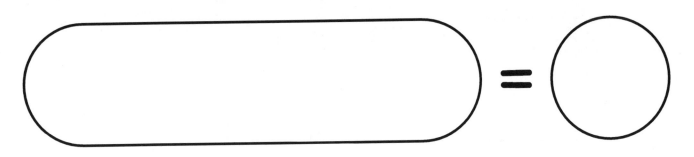

A bakery has 5 trays of cookies. Each tray has 4 cookies. How many cookies are there in the bakery in total?

If a store has 6 shelves of books, and each shelf contains 5 books, how many books does the store have in total?

$$\left(\quad\quad\quad\quad \right) = \bigcirc$$

If a baker has 8 loaves of bread, and each loaf weighs 2 pounds, how much does the baker have in total?

$$\left(\quad\quad\quad\quad \right) = \bigcirc$$

A store sells 11 t-shirts for $3 each. How much money does the store make selling all of the t-shirts?

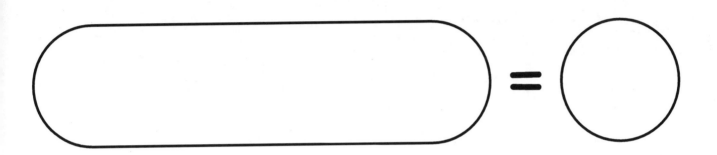

( ) = ( )

If a class has 14 students and each student needs 3 pencils, how many pencils are needed for the entire class?

( ) = ( )

A person earns $5 per hour and works for 8 hours per day. How much money do they earn in a day?

$$\left(\qquad\right) = \bigcirc$$

A factory produces 12 cars per day and it operates for 3 days. How many cars does the factory produce in total?

$$\left(\qquad\right) = \bigcirc$$

If a grocery store has 8 bags of apples, and each bag contains 6 apples, how many apples does the store have in total?

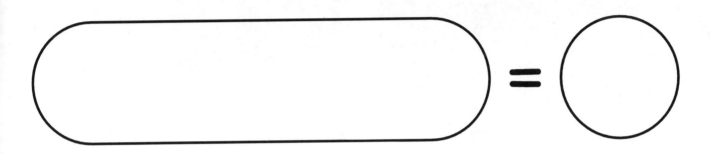

A baker has 4 batches of cookies. Each batch has 6 cookies. How many cookies does the baker have in total?

Other workbooks from our library for your 2nd grader

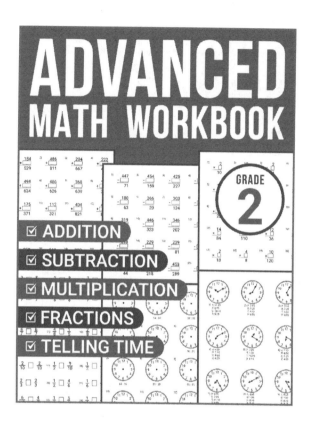

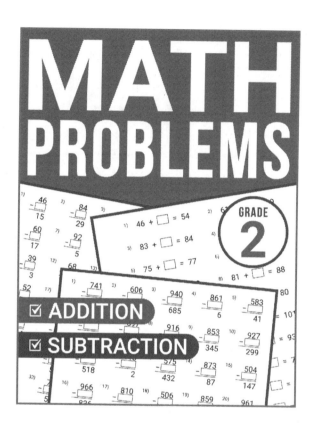

Scan the QR code below:

Scan the QR code below:

www.Nermilio.com

Made in the USA
Columbia, SC
04 November 2024

45646220R00057